Animals

by Barbara Raue
2013

Series Name: The Life and Times of Barbara

Volume 7: Animals

Cover Picture: Flamingoes

Other Books by Barbara Raue

Coins of Gold

Arrows, Indians and Love

The Life and Times of Barbara
Volume 1: Inventions That Have Enhanced My Life
Volume 2: Entertainment That I Have Enjoyed
Volume 3: East Coast Trips
Volume 4: Olympics
Volume 5: Wonders of the World
Volume 6: Caribbean Cruises
Volume 7: Animals

Photography Books by Barbara Raue

Series Name: Cruising Ontario

Book 1: London
Book 2: Dundas
Book 3: Hamilton
Book 4: Oakville
Book 5: Chesley
Book 6: Stoney Creek
Book 7: Waterdown
Book 8: Owen Sound
Book 9: Mount Forest
Book 10: Dundalk
Book 11: Burford and Area
Book 12: Waterford and Area
Book 13: Drumbo and Area
Book 14: Sheffield and Area
Book 15: Tavistock and Area
Book 16: Ancaster and Mount Hope
Book 17: Innerkip and Area
Book 18: Brantford
Book 19: Burlington
Book 20: Guelph and Moffat

I have always enjoyed seeing animals at zoos, but just seeing them is never enough for me. I always want to learn about them, where they live in the wild, what food they eat, how many young they have, what are their enemies, what colours are they. With the internet, it is much easier to do research to learn scientific names and all the details about them. Some animals we have seen many times at various locations; others are specific to a particular park. Here I will share some interesting facts about animals, birds and butterflies.

Peterborough Riverview Park and Zoo

Several times when our boys were young we stopped at the Peterborough Riverview Park and Zoo on our way to our campsite on Buckhorn Lake. The zoo has 27 exhibits, with Yak, Camel, Wallaby (smaller than a kangaroo), Emu, Macaw (brightly coloured parrots), Squirrel Monkey, Cougar, Plated Lizard, Meerkat (a small mammal belonging to the mongoose family) and more. The park on the Otonabee River covers 55.5 acres with walking trails, a miniature train ride, and beautiful gardens.

A century ago, Bald Eagles were a common sight around the Great Lakes, feeding on live or dead fish, aquatic birds, smaller mammals, amphibians and reptiles. Bald Eagles nest in tall trees in enormous nests made of sticks and weeds. They lay from one to three eggs. The eagle is revered by all First Nations people throughout North America as a symbol of protection, vision and wisdom. Bald Eagles live across Canada near major rivers, lakes and sea coasts.

I attended the girls group called Pilgrims from 1957 to 1960. I worked on badges on a regular basis throughout each year. In 1960, when I was nine, I was given a trip to the Pioneer Girls Camp in the United States. From 1961 to 1965, I attended Colonists. For my cooking badge one year, I made a Brazil Nut Torte. I didn't let it cool enough before I put the whipping cream between the layers and it melted the cream. Mom bought all the ingredients I needed so that I could make another one. Another time I made cookies that were not all uniform in size – that is still not a priority for me! Another badge I worked on was about birds, learning what they looked like and the songs they sang, a beginning introduction to learning more about the common birds in our area such as the robin, Baltimore oriole, cardinal, blue jay, and crow. Again in 1965 I was given a trip to Camp for one week. I enjoyed singing songs such as "Grandfather's Clock", and "Land of the Silver Birch".

In July 1984 we made a trip north to visit the Daveys in New Liskeard. Zane, Michael and I enjoyed riding on the horse named Sugar. Swimming in their pool was enjoyable on the warm days. Harry helped with the haying. On our return trip on the way south, we stopped at the Trappers' Museum. I enjoyed the display of stuffed wild animals (bear, beaver, mink, muskrat, flicker woodpecker, ptarmigan, lynx, bobcat, raccoon, and red squirrel). We drove on to Sturgeon Falls on Lake Nipissing and camped for the night. Lake Nipissing is very shallow for a long way out. Harry hooked up Annette's jolly jumper from a tree and she enjoyed a good jump. We spent a day in Sudbury at "Science North" where we saw a beautiful 3-D movie about the Northland. We saw a wizard show, rocks and minerals display, optical illusion display, a twenty-five minute movie, "The Predators," displays showing how weather is formed, experiments on air pressure, fossils, butterfly/moth/insect displays. We camped next at Mikesew Provinical Park on Eagle Lake, west of South River, enjoying the water and sand at the beach. Annette especially liked the sand, eating a lot of it.

Mosaiculture Garden and Butterfly Garden

On Fathers' Day, June 16, 2002 we joined Bob and Hylia MacInnis for a visit to the Niagara Falls Greenhouses, and the Mosaiculture Garden where large ducks, a cat with a ball of string to play with, pony, moose with some Inuit (Eskimo) and caribou nearby, and an elephant were made out of plants. Mosaiculture is a horticultural form of expression in which works of art are made using living plants. It requires the use of several varieties of plants in different colours to create designs. This garden was only open one year.

We concluded the day with a visit to the Butterfly Garden. The richest diversity of butterflies is found in the tropics. The average life span of a butterfly is two to three weeks, with the exception of migrating species like the Monarch which can live for six months. Most butterflies feed on nectar from flowers. The powder on the wings of butterflies is scales that make the colours and patterns and give strength to the wings. Colours and patterns are used as protection, camouflaging them as they blend into their surroundings.

The Mallard ducks are caught in different stages as they begin their flight off the pond

Mountsberg Conservation Area

Mountsberg Conservation Area is in the Burlington area. The birds on display are non-releasable because of permanent injury or other disability. They are housed here to assist in education programs under special federal and provincial permits. The resident birds are provided with the food and shelter they need with choices of low or high perches, shade or sun, rain or shine.

Birds of Prey are carnivorous, meat-eating birds highly adapted to detect, catch and consume the prey species they hunt for. Birds of Prey include mostly day-time active birds, as well as the nocturnal or night-time active owls. Raptor is another term used to describe Birds of Prey as a group. The word raptor comes from a Latin word, raptare, meaning to seize or plunder. All raptors share three main characteristics: keen eyesight, eight sharp talons, and a hooked beak.

In North America, raptors are divided into three main groups or orders: Falconiformes are diurnal (daytime) hunters and include Hawks, Eagles, Harriers, Kites, Falcons, Caracaras and Osprey. Strigiformes, the owls, are mostly nocturnal (night time) hunters. Ciconiiformes includes families such as Storks, Bitterns, and Herons and they are called new world vultures.

Because most owls are nocturnal, their lives and habits are not easy for us to observe. Owls are easily recognized by their large rounded heads and huge, forward-facing eyes. They have a sharply hooked beak and soft coloured plumage. Exceptional vision and acute hearing play a major role in the hunting technique of an owl. Their powerful talons and their ability to fly silently, make the owl a formidable predator. After feeding, owls like other raptors, regurgitate "pellets" that contain the undigested bones, fur and feathers of their previous meal. The smallest owl in the world is the Least Pygmy Owl at 4.5" tall, while the tallest owl is the Great Grey Owl at 33" tall.

The Snowy Owl male is almost all white, while the female is white with black barring and spotting. It prefers lowland tundra with perches on rocks and posts and is seldom seen in trees. It feeds almost exclusively on lemmings and voles, with rats, mice, moles, rabbits, pheasant, quail, and waterfowl occasionally eaten.

The plumage of the Barred Owl is heavily barred with white, black and brown. Its call sounds like the words "who cooks for you, who cooks for you all." It prefers mature mixed woodlands, hunting along wood edges. It eats a variety of small mammals and birds and will also eat frogs, salamanders, small snakes, fish and insects.

The Long Eared Owl has brown and buff plumage with mottling and barring over most of the body. It prefers open woodlands, forest edges, hedgerows and ravines, and may roost communally in dense woods in winter. It eats small mammals such as mice, voles, chipmunks, shrews and rabbits, as well as small birds, insects and frogs.

The Barn Owl has tawny and grey upper parts with small black and white spots and white under parts. It likes open countryside with grassland, marshland, hedgerows and woodland edges. It eats rodents such as mice, rats, voles and shrews, and will catch small birds in winter.

Falcons have fascinated humans for centuries with their aerial grace and skill. Under their keen eyes, most falcons have a teardrop marking called a "malar stripe". The bill is short, powerful, and has a distinct "tooth" on each side which is used to dispatch prey. Falcons are fast flying birds of the open country and are famous for attaining speeds of over 300 kilometres per hour as they "stoop dive" from high altitudes to knock other birds out of the air.

The Peregrine Falcon has a dark, slate coloured crown and upper surface of the wings, the throat is white and under parts are white to buff with blackish brown bars on the sides, thighs, abdomen, under wings and lower breast area. They eat birds such as ducks, gulls, terns, shorebirds, and pigeons and will catch small mammals.

The male American Kestrel has bluish wings and brown breast, while the female has brown wings and streaked breast. They prefer open grassland with some trees, forest edges, and suburban parks. Their diet consists of insects, small birds, mammals and reptiles.

The Turkey Vulture is a common sight in southern Ontario and is the only species of vulture native to this area. They spend much of their time soaring high above the ground, searching for food with their highly developed sense of smell and excellent eyesight. Turkey vultures play an important role in our ecosystem and act as a "clean-up crew". Vultures are carrion eaters, unlike other raptors who prefer to catch and kill their own prey. They can often be seen along roadsides cleaning up road-kill, or feasting on washed-up fish near waterways. Turkey Vultures can be identified in flight because they hold their wings in a shallow "V" shape and the primary flight feathers at the ends of the wings tend to resemble "fingers".

Eagles are large, powerful birds of prey that use soaring or sprinting flight to hunt. These magnificent raptors are regarded as living symbols of power, beauty and freedom. Eagles have large powerful hooked beaks, talons and keen eyesight. The Bald Eagle prefers mixed hardwood forests close to water. They eat fish, occasionally mammals, birds and carrion.

Wood ducks symbolize the intrinsic value of wetlands. These beautiful birds, with green crested heads and red eyes, nest in tree cavities or man-made nesting boxes located in the wooded swamps of Mountsberg. The female is remarkably agile in getting in and out of tight places. Ten to fifteen eggs are laid in the spring and incubated for about 30 days. When the ducklings hatch, they must get down to the ground or the water to feed as the young birds cannot fly for several months. The female first appears out of the nesting cavity to ensure that no danger is near. She then flies to the ground and calls with a soft and prolonged pe-ee pe-ee sound. Seconds later a chorus of peeping cries can be heard from the nest. This is followed by a burst of fluffy down as ten or more ducklings jump out of the hole and fall to the ground.

Marineland

We have visited Marineland many times over the years. Here are some interesting facts about some of the animals we have seen. What marvellous variety we have to admire.

Black Bears are native to North America, varying in size depending on their sex, age and the time of the year. Adult Black Bears can weigh five hundred pounds and they vary in colour from a solid jet black to light brown to chocolate or a bluish grey. At Marineland, their diet consists of fish, meat, vegetables and fruits. Black Bears love sweets such as honey and marshmallows.

The Red Deer earned its name because of its beautiful reddish-brown coat. The deer's under parts are lighter and there is a white patch under the tail. The winter coat is long, brittle and more of a greyish-brown colouration. As the deer's main defense against enemies is to flee, the animal is perfectly built for this having long legs, excellent vision and a keen sense of smell to assist the animal in detecting and escaping danger. The male with a full set of antlers makes him a most impressive sight. The antlers are usually branched in a complex manner with six to ten points on each branch. The antlers are supported by a long, strong neck.

The deer is native to Europe and can be found living in a wide variety of habitats from dense forests to moors, from flood plains and lowlands to plateaus and the Alps. Once established in an area, the Red Deer will multiply quickly, which often results in a shortage of food. Regardless of a shortage, the deer will put their numbers at risk rather than move to another area with a more abundant food supply. Red Deer spend most of their time feeding. The rest of their time is spent ruminating and resting and sleeping, but only briefly. Red Deer feed primarily on herbs, grasses and small plants. In the winter months when this type of food is scarce, the deer will eat conifer needles, lichens, softwood bark and grass that they scrape from under the snow. The Red Deer also greatly restrict their movement during the winter to conserve energy.

The Algonquin name Wapiti, commonly referred to as Elk in North America, is the largest of the deer family. The Wapiti is up to nine feet long in head and body, resembling the Red Deer in colour except it is less reddish in summer and it has a prominent light rump patch. The antlers of a Wapiti may reach 66 inches above its head. The Wapiti is an herbivorous animal, eating fruit and vegetables, as well as alfalfa, hay, corn, oats and barley.

The two species of bison alive today are the European bison and the American bison, often called buffalo. Bison live in herds, are most active during the morning and evening, and are fond of wallowing in mud and rubbing themselves against trees and boulders. The Plains Bison of the United States is smaller and lighter in colour than the Wood Bison of Canada, and has a heavier head and rump. Despite its enormous and clumsy appearance, the bison is a surprisingly agile and sure-footed creature. Bulls can grow ten or twelve feet in length and as tall as six feet at the shoulder, weighing 3,000 pounds. The bison can swim very well. The hair on the head, neck, shoulders and forelegs is long and shaggy. The forehead is broad and is flanked by two short, curving horns that are carried by both sexes. The hair on the head can grow up to one foot long and forms a beard on the chins of the bulls.

When Europeans first settled in North America, bison could be found from northern Canada as far south as the border of Mexico, and across the continent from the east to the Rockies. They were hunted so relentlessly that they nearly became extinct. The future of the North American Bison is now more secure by being preserved through game farms and reserves like Marineland. The North American Bison is herbivorous feeding mainly on grass. At Marineland, the main diet consists of hay, corn, oats, barley and water.

Killer Whales reach a length of 30 feet and weigh up to 16,000 pounds. The dorsal fin of an adult male reaches a height of six feet. Male Killer Whales live up to 50 years while females live from 80 to 100 years. Killer Whales travel in pods and are found throughout all oceans of the world in the offshore and inshore waters. In North America, the Killer Whale is found mainly in the Puget Sound, Washington state area and off the coast of Vancouver Island, British Columbia.

Female orcas carry their calves from 16-18 months. Calves are usually born fluke first as opposed to land animals which are more often born head first. The birth of a calf occurs rapidly, which is necessary because the young must surface for its first breath soon after the umbilical cord breaks; otherwise it would die of anoxia. When the whale is ready to give birth, it is sometimes seen spiraling under the water's surface working with the force of water and gravity to expel the calf. A new calf weighs approximately 150 pounds and is 6 feet long. The mother quickly guides the newborn to its first breath of air and swims alongside her calf protecting it from intruders and danger. Nursing begins shortly after birth and continues for about 1 year. After approximately 2½ months, the nursing periods become shorter and the calf starts receiving solid fish from its mother to supplement the milk received while nursing.

Killer Whales use their 48 cone-shaped teeth to grasp and tear their food which they do not chew but swallow whole. Large Killer Whales eat up to 125 pounds per day. Killer Whales have no natural enemies. Most of the Killer Whale's body is black with white eye patches and a white underside. There is a light grey area behind the dorsal fin called the saddle. The Killer Whale's striking colour pattern is called "disruptive camouflage" and aids the Killer Whale in hunting its prey by allowing it to blend into its ocean environment.

Beluga Whales are born brownish-gray in colour with fine dark spots, but they slowly lose this pigmentation as they age. Upon reaching maturity, they are yellowish to creamy white. Beluga Whales inhabit shallow waters very close to the ice that covers the Arctic Ocean. They are vocal marine mammals producing a wide range of sounds that can be described as squeals, chirps, whistles, clicks and screeches. Belugas use their 34 peg-shaped teeth to grasp their food which consists of capelin, herring, salmon, cod, flounder, squid, shrimp, crabs, snails and worms. They hunt schools of fish and forage under ice and on the ocean floor. Like most cetaceans, Belugas do not chew their food but swallow it whole. The adult males will eat 35-60 pounds per day, and the females 25-45 pounds. A fully grown male ranges from 13-16 feet in length and weighs 3,300 pounds.

Female Belugas carry their calves 14-15 months. Belugas breed March through May with calves being born either head or tail first in April through September. On average, calves are 5 feet in length and weigh 175 pounds, and calves nurse for 20-24 months. Once they have teeth, the calf will also eat small fish and shrimp.

The seven neck vertebrae of Beluga whales are not fused, allowing the whale greater range of head and neck motion. The forehead region of the Beluga is hangs out over the snout. The species name for Belugas is *Delphinapterus leucas,* which means "the white dolphin without a wing". It was given this name because it is one of the few cetaceans that lack a wing-like dorsal fin on its back. A dorsal fin would limit their ability to swim under the ice found in their Arctic habitat. Sometimes they ram their backs upwards against the surface ice in order to break through for a breath of air. A dorsal fin would make that impossible, while their stiff dorsal ridge proves to be an ideal ice breaker.

Beluga Whale

Matthew watching the seagulls

African Lion Safari

Another popular place to visit is the African Lion Safari. There are many varieties of animals to see beginning in the Nairobi Sanctuary. Ankole-Watusi is a breed of cattle native to Africa with very large, distinctive horns similar to a Texas Longhorn.

The llama is a South American herbivorous camelid widely used as a pack animal by the Incas and other natives of the Andes mountains. The height of a full-grown llama is between 5½ and 6 feet and they weigh between 280 and 450 pounds. At birth, a baby llama weighs between 20 and 30 pounds. The fiber produced by a llama is very soft and naturally lanolin free. When using a pack, llamas can carry 25%–30% of their body weight for several miles.

European White Storks are tall long-necked wading birds with long bare red legs and a straight pointed red bill. The white plumage of the head, neck, and body contrasts with the black wing feathers highlighted with a sheen of purple and green iridescence. The contour feathers of the lower neck and chest are elongated to form a fluffy ruff that can be erected during courtship displays. A small patch of bare black skin surrounds their brown eyes.

The East African Grey-necked Crowned Crane is three feet tall, weighs about eight pounds, and has a gray body. The wings are predominantly white, but contain feathers with colors ranging from white to brown to gold. The head is topped with a crown of stiff golden feathers. All crowned cranes have the ability to perch because their long hind toe allows for grasping.

The Griffon Vulture is an Old World vulture, about forty inches long with a 100 inch wingspan, and weighs between 13 and 29 pounds. It has a white bald head, very broad wings, a short tail, a white neck ruff and yellow bill. The buff body and wing coverts contrast with the dark flight feathers. It is a scavenger, feeding mostly from carcasses of dead animals which it finds by soaring over open areas. It grunts and hisses at roosts or when feeding on carrion.

The Simba Lion Country is the next reserve. Lions are the only cats that live in groups called prides, family units that may include up to three males, a dozen females, and their young. All of a pride's lionesses are related, and female cubs typically stay with the group as they age. Young males eventually leave and establish their own prides by taking over a group headed by another male. Only male lions have manes, the impressive fringe of long hair that encircles their heads. Males defend the pride's territory, which may include 100 square miles of grasslands, scrub, or open woodlands. Female lions are the pride's primary hunters working together to prey upon antelopes, zebras, wildebeest, and other large animals of the open grasslands.

Many of these animals are faster than lions, so teamwork pays off. After the hunt, the group effort often degenerates to squabbling over the sharing of the kill, with cubs at the bottom of the pecking order. Young lions do not help to hunt until they are about a year old. Today lions are found in parts of sub-Saharan Africa, with one small population of Asian lions surviving in India's Gir Forest.

In Duma Cheetah Preserve, the cheetahs are seen prowling along the fences. The cheetah is a member of the cat family that is unique in its speed, while lacking climbing abilities. It is the fastest land animal, reaching speeds between 70 and 75 mph in short bursts covering distances up to 1,500 feet, and has the ability to accelerate from 0 to 68 mph in three seconds, greater than most supercars.

On the Wankie Bushland Trail, the baboons are busy playing, feeding, and climbing on the vehicles slowly wending their way along the trail. The Chacma Baboon is South Africa's largest wild primate. This primate is omnivorous (eats plants and meat) but prefers to be herbivorous (eating plant-like material). The hair colouration of the Savannah Baboon can come in all forms, from dark grey to a greyish-brown colour while the hands and feet are a light black colour. The baby and juvenile Baboons have black coats and pinkish faces. The Chacma Baboon is found throughout South Africa in mountainous regions with tall trees.

The Rocky Ridge Veldt is a large area with animals native to Africa. The trail takes a large loop around the veldt and many kinds of animals are found together in groups, while others are only with their own species. The Greater Kudu is a woodland antelope found throughout eastern and southern Africa. They have a narrow body with long legs, and their coats range from brown/bluish-grey to reddish-brown. They have between four and twelve vertical white stripes along their torso. The head tends to be darker in colour than the rest of the body, and exhibits a small white chevron which runs between the eyes. The males have large manes running along their throats, and large horns with two and a half twists, which, were they to be straightened, would reach an average length of three feet. The male horns begin to grow when the male is between six and twelve months, twisting once at two years of age, and reaching the full two and a half twists when they are six years old. Females do not have horns.

The giraffe is an African even-toed hoofed mammal, the tallest of all land-living animal species, and the largest ruminant (chews the cud). Males can be 16 to 18 feet tall and weigh up to 3,800 pounds. Giraffes inhabit savannas, grasslands, and open woodlands preferring areas enriched with acacia growth. They drink large quantities of water and, as a result, can spend long periods of time in dry, arid areas.

The Grant's Zebra is the smallest of the Plains Zebra. Zebras are odd-toed ungulates (hoofed) native to eastern, southern and south western Africa. They are best known for their distinctive white and black stripes. Zebras are eight feet long, stand four to five feet at the shoulder, and weigh around 660 pounds. Zebras have erect, mohawk-like manes. They can be found in a variety of habitats, such as grasslands, savannas, woodlands, thorny scrublands, mountains and coastal hills. The name "zebra" comes from the Old Portuguese word *zevra* which means "wild ass".

The Blue Wildebeest or Brindled Gnu is a large hoofed mammal which grows to 5½ feet at shoulder height and weighs up to 840 pounds. They are grazing antelope that live in huge herds on the plains of Africa having a life span over twenty years. The name "Blue Wildebeest" derives from a conspicuous silvery blue sheen to the short haired hide with a slatey grey coat, a black tail, and a long narrow head carrying horns which curve down and then up. In the male the horns can attain a total span of 35 inches, while the female's horn width is about half the size. The front quarters are heavily built and there is a mane and a beard reaching down the throat.

The Common or Southern Eland is a savannah and plains antelope found in East and Southern Africa standing four feet at the shoulder, the world's largest antelope. Females have a tan coat, while males have a darker tan coat with a bluish-grey tinge; there may also be a series of white stripes vertically on the sides of bulls. Males have dense fur on their foreheads and a large flap of skin that hangs beneath the lower jaw. Both sexes have horns, about 26 inches long with a spiral ridge.

The Barbary Sheep is a species of goat-antelope found in rocky mountains in North Africa and has been introduced to North America and southern Europe. Barbary Sheep stand thirty to forty inches tall at the shoulder and weigh 90 to 300 pounds. They are a sandy-brown colour, darkening with age, with a slightly lighter underbelly and a darker line on the back. Upperparts and outer legs are uniform reddish-brown or grayish-brown. There is some shaggy hair on the throat extending down to the chest in males and a sparse mane. Their horns, having a triangular cross section, curve outwards, backwards then inwards, and reach up to twenty inches. The horns are smooth, but wrinkled at the base.

The Ostrich is a large flightless bird native to Africa, has a long neck and legs and the ability to run at speeds of 46 miles per hour, the top land speed of any bird. The Ostrich is the largest species of bird and lays the largest egg of any bird species. The diet consists of plant matter and insects. When threatened, the Ostrich will either hide itself by lying flat against the ground, or will run away. If cornered, it can cause injury and death with a kick from its powerful legs. The Ostrich is farmed around the world for its feathers which are decorative and also used for feather dusters. Its skin is used for leather and its meat marketed commercially.

The White Rhinoceros or Square-lipped rhinoceros is one of the five species of rhinoceros that still exist. Behind only the Elephant, it is the most massive land animal in the world. It has a wide mouth for grazing. This rhino weighs 8,000 pounds, has a head-and-body length of 11 to 14 feet and a shoulder height of 5 to 6 feet. On its snout it has two horns made of keratin (the main constituent of structures that grow from the skin), rather than bone as in deer antlers. The front horn is larger than the other horn and averages 35 inches in length. The White Rhinoceros has a noticeable hump on the back of its neck which supports its large head. Each of the rhino's four stumpy feet has three toes. Its colour ranges from yellowish brown to slate grey. The only hair is on the ear fringes and tail bristles.

Eurasia is the area where animals from Europe and Asia are found. The Himalayan Tahr is a large hoofed animal, a close relative of the wild goat. Its native habitat is in the rugged wooded hills and mountain slopes of the Himalaya from northern India to Tibet. They spend the summers grazing in high pastures, then come down the mountains and form herds in the winter. The dense, woolly winter coat is reddish to dark brown and has a thick undercoat. With their winter coat, males also grow a long, shaggy mane around the neck and shoulders which extends down the front legs. After the spring moult, the coat is much shorter and lighter in colour. The legs are short and the head is small with large eyes and small, pointed ears. The horns are triangular in cross-section and are found in both sexes. They curve upward, backwards, and then inwards, to a length of eighteen inches.

The Tibetan Yak is a long-haired bovine found throughout the Himalayan region of south Central Asia. Male yaks stand seven feet tall at the shoulder, and have long shaggy hair to insulate them from the cold. Wild yaks can be brown or black while domesticated ones can also be white. Both males and females have horns.

The Nilgai is an antelope commonly seen in northern India and eastern Pakistan. The mature males appear ox-like and are also known as Blue Bulls. The Nilgai is the biggest Asian antelope standing 4 to 5 feet at the shoulder and 6 to 6½ feet long with tails 16 to 18 inches long. Nilgai have thin legs and a robust body that slopes down from the shoulder. Their long, narrow heads are topped by two small conical horns which are straight and tilted slightly forward and 8½ to 10 inches long. They have an erectile mane on the back of the neck and a tubular shaped "hair pennant" on the midsection of the throat.

The Mouflon male has long tightly coiled horns. The Mouflon is a handsome looking sheep with a short, shiny coat that has a rich red or dark brown colour. The winter coat is much thicker than the summer coat; the Mouflon moults twice a year. It is the smallest of the wild sheep species, with a height of only 3 to 3½ feet and weighs 55 to 110 pounds.

The Japanese Sika Deer inhabits much of East Asia and is found in mixed deciduous forests to the north, and mixed subtropical deciduous and evergreen forests to the south. The colour of the coat ranges from greyish or chestnut brown to reddish olive, with the chin, belly, and throat being off-white. Their coat grows shaggier in the winter, forming a dark mane on the neck, especially in males. On the rump, an erectile patch of light-colour is used as a warning signal. The males grow antlers that are narrow and erect with two to ten tines on each bar, measuring 1 to 2½ feet in length.

The Sicilian Donkey is a miniature breed of domestic donkey standing 28 to 38 inches tall at the withers. They weigh between 250 and 450 pounds. The most common colour is gray, but they range from black, brown, chestnut, white, or spotted. The Sicilian breed is noted for a cross-shaped marking along the back beginning at the base of the neck.

The Turkmenian Markhor is a goat-antelope found in sparse woodlands in the Western Himalayas. Markhor stand 25 to 45 inches at the shoulder and weigh from 90 to 240 pounds. Females are tan in colour with a white underbelly and a pattern of black and white on the legs. Males have a lighter tan colour with the same white underbelly and pattern on the legs, as well as a black face and a large amount of long shaggy white fur on their neck and chest which can grow to knee-length. Both sexes have corkscrew-shaped horns which can grow up to 64 inches long in males, but only ten inches in females. Markhor are found at altitudes of 1,500 to 11,000 feet where they eat grass, leaves, and other vegetative matter they can find, often standing on their hind legs to reach the top leaves of trees.

We took a trip on the African Queen boat with Sam, Annette, Michael, Grace and Matthew. Sam is not comfortable on the water but he joined us as we travelled around the islands with monkeys inhabiting them. Each of our children and grandchildren, our gems, is different making a colourful and valuable pouch.

The Black-handed Spider Monkey has a prehensile tail which it uses for grasping when feeding and when moving through the forest. It is found in forests and evergreen tropical rainforests, preferring to live in the upper levels of the canopy. It is found in the countries of Belize, Costa Rica, El Salvador, Guatemala, Honduras, Mexico, Nicaragua, and Panama. The black-handed spider monkey is a frugivorous species favouring ripe fruits, and leaves.

The White-handed Gibbon, like the gorilla, chimpanzee and orangutan, is an ape, not a monkey. Gibbons are very small and lightweight with a small, round head, very long arms (the arms are longer than the legs), and a short, slender body. The long forearms assist it in suspensory behaviour. Gibbons are arboreal, spending most of their lives in trees. They are covered with light-colored to very dark brown (or black) dense hair on most of their body. The fur provides protection from rain.

The Black and White Ruffed Lemur can grow up to four feet long, but they only weigh eight or ten pounds. Both males and females look the same, with black and white markings and a ruff of long white fur around their ears and neck. These lemurs live in the eastern rainforests of Madagascar and eat fruit and other plants.

The Marabou Stork is a large wading bird which lives in Africa south of the Sahara in both wet and arid habitats, often near human habitation. It is sometimes called the "undertaker bird," due to its shape from behind: cloak-like wings and back, skinny white legs, and sometimes a large white mass of "hair." The Marabou Stork is a scavenger, and the naked head and neck are great for this – a feathered head would become rapidly clotted with blood and other substances when the bird's head was inside a large corpse – the bare head is easier to keep clean. This large and powerful bird will eat different kinds of animals, either alive or as carrion, including small mammals and reptiles. Living prey includes termites, fish, locusts, grasshoppers, caterpillars, frogs, rodents, crocodile eggs and hatchlings, doves, young and adult flamingos, cormorant nestlings, and pelican chicks.

The Southern Ground-Hornbill is a large bird, 35 to 50 inches long and weighs 7 to 13 pounds. It is characterized by black coloration and vivid red patches of bare skin on the face and throat. The white tips of the wings (primary feathers) seen in flight are another characteristic. They live in savannahs, woodlands and grasslands in northern Namibia, Angola, northern South Africa, Burundi and Kenya.

The Ring-tailed Lemur is found only on the island of Madagascar where it inhabits evergreen forests along rivers or wetlands and in landscapes that are sparsely treed. In addition to being active during the day time and resting at night, it is mostly terrestrial, living on the ground. The Ring-tailed Lemur is widely recognized and easily distinguished from other lemur species by its long, black and white ringed tail. It primarily eats fruits and leaves, particularly those of the tamarind tree.

The Emu is the largest bird native to Australia. The soft-feathered, flightless birds reach up to 6½ feet in height. Emus can travel great distances at a fast, economical trot and, if necessary, can sprint at 30 mph. They have brown to grey-brown plumage of shaggy appearance; the shafts and the tips of the feathers are black. They eat a variety of plant species as well as insects such as grasshoppers, crickets, lady birds, soldier and saltbush caterpillars, Bogong and cotton-ball moth larvae and ants.

The Tufted Capuchin Monkey is a primate from South America. It is an omnivorous animal, eating both plants and animals. It uses stones as a tool to open hard nuts. First it lays the nut on a large, flat stone and then it hammers with a smaller stone until the nut is opened. It eats fruit, insects, larvae, eggs, young birds, frogs, lizards, and bats. It is found in moist tropical and subtropical forest, dry forest, and disturbed or secondary forest.

Spider monkeys are named because of their long, spidery limbs. Their prehensile tail acts like a fifth limb when swinging through the canopy and is used to pick up items as small as sunflower seeds. Spider monkeys live in the tropical rain forests of Central and South America and Mexico. They are active during the day. Their coat colour varies from light buff to black with black hands and feet.

The Angolan Black and White Colobus Monkeys have black hair with a white brow band, cheeks, and throat. Long haired white epaulettes stream from the shoulders. The lower part of the tail is white as is the band on the buttocks. These monkeys are only found in the southern Kenyan coastal forests and the northern Tanzanian highlands. This monkey is primarily a folivorous species eating leaves, but it also consumes termite clay, fruits, and flowers.

The Black Swan is a large water bird which breeds in the southeast and southwest regions of Australia. They have mostly black feathers with a line of white flight feathers on the wing edges that sometimes show when at rest but are conspicuous in flight. The bill is bright red, with a pale bar and tip. When swimming, Black Swans hold their necks arched or erect, and often carry their feathers or wings raised in an aggressive display. In flight, a wedge of Black Swans will form as a line or a V, with the individual birds flying strongly with undulating long necks, making whistling sounds with their wings and baying, bugling or trumpeting calls.

Flamingoes

Our youngest gem, Matthew, enjoyed a pony ride. Then we all took a trip on the Nature Boy Scenic Railway for beautiful scenery and more animals to see such as llamas, Fallow Deer, Dromedary Camel, Bactrian Camel, Reindeer, and Caribbean Flamingo. The Pets' Corner was a fun place to spend some time with the alpaca, camel, and goats, followed by a trip to the Funnel Cake Factory for a treat.

There were several kinds of Parrots to view including the African Grey Parrot, Scarlet Macaw, Blue and Gold Macaw, Military Macaw, Buffon Macaw, Hyacinthe Macaw, Green-winged Macaw, Catelina Macaw, Umbrella, Moluccan Cockatoo, Galah Cockatoo, Alexandrine Parakeet, Princess of Wales Parakeet, Channel Billed Toucan, Red Billed Toucan, Victoria Crowned Pigeon, and Rainbow Macaw. What bright jewel-tone colours they have!

The Birds of Prey were our next stop. Bald Eagles, found throughout North America, often build nests in trees and over the course of many seasons their nests can grow to an enormous size, weighing as much as a ton. Bald Eagles are found near lakes, marshes, rivers and coastal areas preying mostly on fish and waterfowl and sometimes scavenge on carrion. Bald Eagles live 15 to 20 years in the wild and up to 50 years in captivity.

The average flight speed of Golden Eagles is 30 miles per hour but they can reach speeds up to 90 miles per hour when diving down on their prey. Golden Eagles prefer wide open spaces in mountainous country preying upon a wide variety of mammals and game birds. The beak is well suited to tear apart large prey. In the wild, Golden Eagles live about 17 years. These birds are widespread throughout the Northern Hemisphere.

The African Fish Eagle is a large bird of prey. Males have a wingspan of about six feet, while females have wingspans of more than eight feet. They have a brown body and large, powerful, black wings. The head, breast, and tail are snow white and the hook-shaped beak is yellow with a black tip. It feeds mainly on fish, which, upon spying it from a perch in a tree, it will swoop down upon and snatch from the water with its large clawed talons and fly back to its perch to eat. Should the African Fish Eagle catch a fish over four pounds it will be too heavy to allow it to get lift, so it will drag the fish across the surface of the water until it reaches the shore. If it catches a fish that is too heavy to even allow the eagle to sustain flight, it will drop into the water and paddle to the nearest shore with its wings. It is amazing how each bird and animal is uniquely adapted for the way it lives.

Other birds of prey to see were the Tawny Eagle, Peregrine Falcon, Red-tailed Hawk, Great Black Hawk, Harris' Hawk, Ferruginous Hawk, Snowy Owl, Eurasian Eagle Owl, Barn Owl, Spectacled Owl, Great Horned Owl, Burrowing Owl, Black Vulture, King Vulture, Turkey Vulture, Cinereous Vulture (Eurasian Black Vulture), and Indian Peafowl.

There is a very large variety of animals and birds to see at the African Lion Safari. I have included pictures of only a few.

The Asian Elephants put on a lovely show for us.

Elephant Trust

Jumbo

Jumbo, a young African elephant, was sold to the Paris Zoo and later to the London Zoo where he remained for 17 years and reached his great size and endeared himself with his gentle ways to members of the Royal Family and hundreds of thousands of English children that he carried on his broad back. P.T. Barnum purchased Jumbo for $10,000, although the Queen and millions of Britons, young and old, unsuccessfully attempted to prevent the sale of their beloved Jumbo. Upon his arrival in New York, thousands thronged the docks and lined Broadway as he was carted down the street. Jumbo toured America with the Barnum and Bailey Circus. He struck up a friendship with the diminutive clown elephant Tom Thumb and the two animals won the hearts of millions as they went from town to town. On September 15, 1885, in St. Thomas, Ontario, Jumbo and Tom Thumb were being led back along the tracks to their circus railway car after the evening performance, when an unscheduled Grand Trunk train suddenly appeared out of the fog. Jumbo and Tom Thumb were trapped between the parked circus train and a steep bank which Jumbo refused to descend. As they raced for safety along the track they were overtaken by the train. The locomotive and two cars were derailed. Tom Thumb was hurled down the bank and received a broken leg. Jumbo was thrown forward into the line of the railway cars; a tusk was driven into his brain. As he lay dying in the cinders, he tenderly reached up with his trunk and drew his keeper Scott down to him. It was the end of 20 years of a devoted friendship between a faithful servant and his master. A life size monument of Jumbo was erected in 1985 at the west entrance to St. Thomas to commemorate the 100th anniversary of his fateful visit.

Harry looks very small standing by the statue of Jumbo.

Toronto Zoo

On August 1, 2009 we joined our gems, Michael, Grace, Matthew and Katie for a trip to the Toronto Zoo. We saw polar bears, wolves, reindeer, flamingos, gorillas and monkeys, elephants, zebra and some exotic birds. Conservation is the reason the Toronto Zoo exists and they have over 5,000 animals representing more than 450 species, many of which are threatened or endangered. The zoo, covering an area of 287 hectares (710 acres), opened on August 15, 1974 and is divided into seven zoogeographic regions: Indo-Malaya, Africa, Americas, Tundra Trek, Australasia, Eurasia and the Canadian Domain. Some animals are displayed indoors in tropical pavilions and outdoors in what would be their naturalistic environments.

Sharks and stingrays were interesting to learn about. Sharks have flexible cartilage in place of bones in their bodies; their teeth are constantly replaced; they live in salt or fresh water; and they range in size from 17 centimetres (7 inches) in length to about 12 metres (39 feet).

At the 10 acres Tundra Trek, there are polar bears, white Arctic wolves pacing along the fence, reindeer, snow geese and snowy owls.

The hoof pads of reindeer and caribou are soft and spread wide in the summer to walk more easily on the boggy tundra. In winter, their hoof pads get harder and hair grows between their toes to break ice covering the low-lying plants they eat and to prevent the animals from skidding and slipping on icy surfaces.

Black-footed ferrets with masked eyes and black feet are the only ferrets native to North America. Their primary prey was prairie dogs and when these were exterminated, the ferrets declined in numbers.

Jaguars are the largest wild cat in the Americas measuring up to six feet from the base of the tail to the nose. The black jaguar is not a different species, just a different colour, and it also has spots on its coat.

The spider monkey lives in southern Central America and northern South America. It has a hairless black face with flesh coloured spectacles around the eyes and a body covered with pale coloured bristly fur. Its long limbs and long tail allow the monkey to move fast through the trees.

The American alligator was listed as endangered in 1967 but through strict law enforcement, habitat protection and wise management, they have made a comeback. During periods of drought in the Everglades, alligators dig small ponds to give them access to water below the ground. These alligator holes provide a habitat for aquatic animals and drinking water for many others. The San Esteban Island chuckwalla is an endangered lizard which feeds on flowers, leaves, cactus fruits, berries and insects.

In the African Rainforest Pavilion there is a range from bats and birds to reptiles, amphibians and fish. Due to loss of habitat, poaching, and other threats, gorillas are critically endangered. Gorillas are gentle and peace-loving animals, they are vegetarian, and they love to play in their family groups.

Meerkats are a type of mongoose that lives in the Kalahari Desert in Africa. They dig underground tunnels with up to seventy accesses to escape from eagles and jackals.

The Pygmy Hippopotamus lives in dense, swampy forests and weighs about a quarter of a ton. Logging and clearing the forest for agriculture destroys their habitat. The River Hippo weighs up to four and half tons and is more widely spread throughout Africa than the Pygmy.

In the African Savanna the lynx, cheetah, elephant, kudu, zebra, lions, antelope and rhinoceros are found. The African elephant was poached heavily for its ivory tusks. The elephant uses its tusks for digging, fighting, and for helping a calf up a steep bank.

Zebras are the wild horses of Africa. Some zebras have adapted to mountains, others to drier regions, but most live in the Savanna. The stripes may be a camouflage feature making it more difficult for the lions or hyenas to know where one animal ends and another begins when the zebra herd is on the run.

Hippos need to live where there is enough water to cover their bodies. Staying in water keeps them cool and keeps their skin from burning. At night they graze on the nearby grasslands, eating about 40 kilograms each night.

Without water, nothing lives as water drives the cycle of life. Rain dictates the seasons on the savanna. When the dry season begins, the grasses go dormant, frogs burrow underground, and grazing animals migrate. Thirsty animals gather around dwindling water holes. When the rains come, the pools, lakes, swamps and rivers provide a home for a great variety of waterfowl. The grass grows green, the wildflowers bloom, and wildlife babies are born.

Baboons are bigger, faster and more aggressive than most monkeys. Baboons spend time reinforcing relationships by mutual grooming because cooperation matters when confronted by a leopard.

A caracal is a tawny cat with long legs and elegant ears. They hunt in the early morning and evening usually feeding on rodents and hares, and are particularly good at hunting birds.

In the Australasia Pavilion, we saw tree kangaroos that spend most of their time climbing in the trees of Papua New Guinea. They are threatened by habitat destruction caused by logging and oil and mineral exploration.

A billabong is an Australian Aboriginal word meaning "dead river" and is formed in a flat country where a meandering river cuts through a loop in its own channel and forms a pond or small lake of still water. During the wet season, the billabongs may be flooded by the river and may still contain water when the river runs dry during the dry season. Billabongs are home to many species of amphibians, fish, crayfish, insects and water plants.

We saw birds such as the Australian Magpie, Victoria Crowned Pigeon, Kookabura (I always thought Kookaburas were animals!), parakeets, and the Little Pied Cormorant.

Victoria Crowned Pigeon – a beautiful blue colour

Jellyfish have no bones and are invertebrates related to corals and sea anemones. They are found in every ocean and some freshwater lakes. The body of the jellyfish is like an umbrella and opens and closes helping to move the jelly as it drifts along.

When komodo dragons reach full size they fear nothing. With its great bulk and serrated teeth, a komodo can bring down an adult water buffalo.

Matthew on Komodo

The Siberian Tiger was pacing along the fence for us to enjoy watching.

Kangaroos and wallabies and emus fed on the grasses with the Canada Geese. In the Americas Pavilion the beavers and otters swim; birds such as owls, jays, finches, scarlet-headed blackbird, scarlet ibis, and silver beak tanager are a few of the species; there are amphibians, fish, spiders and crabs; flamingoes, monkeys and macaws are sights to enjoy. The zoo wouldn't be complete without the elk, moose, cougar and grizzly bear.

Niagara Falls Aviary

We took a trip with Bob and Hylia MacInnis to the Niagara Falls Aviary – what unique birds we saw and photographed. My project was not complete until I did research on the birds to learn more about them. Years later we returned to the Aviary with Michael and his family, an opportunity to see the birds from the young children's perspective.

The Yellow-hooded Blackbird is found in the northern countries of South America in marshes and wet grasslands. The head of the bird is a bright yellow while the rest of the body is black.

The Wattled Jacana is a black and brown bird, 20 centimetres in length, with yellow markings on its wings. The bird has big toes so that it can walk over plants in the marshes.

The California Quail likes areas with lots of brush where it feeds on seeds, plant buds, and insects.

The Black-Headed Bulbul is found in Malaysia in lowland forest areas where it feeds on small fruit. It has bright yellow plumage with a black bluish glossy head.

The Red-Headed Parrot Finch is found in New Caledonia, a group of islands located in the southwest Pacific Ocean, east of Australia. The finch is vivacious, energetic doing everything with gusto. It has a red face, upper breast, rump and tail and the rest of the body is parrot green. The finch weighs about 15 grams. It eats various seeds. Like all other Parrot-finches, they love to bathe.

The Gouldian Finch is a colourful bird native to the dry eucalyptus savannas in northern Australia. It has bright purple yellow and green feathers. Gouldians bond and mate for life.

The male Fire Finch has a bright red head, breast, and under parts. This finch is found in Central Ethiopia south to Mozambique, Zimbabwe and Zambia where it feeds on or near the ground on seeds of grasses and other plants.

The Java Sparrow, native to Indonesia, feeds on grain and other seeds, frequenting open grassland and cultivation. The adult is 17 centimetres in length, has grey upperparts and breast, a pink belly, white cheeks with a black head and a thick red bill.

Star Finches, about 13 centimetres tall and 12 centimetres in length, are very colourful and originate from Northern Australia where they live in tropical swamps, rice and sugar-cane fields, dense scrub, woodland trees, and in tall grasses near water. The face and beak are red; the throat, neck and flanks are spotted white; the back, breast and wings are a grey-green to pale olive-green colour; the abdomen is yellow.

Orange-cheeked Waxbill come from Western Africa in open grassland with light tree and/or shrub coverage, also along watercourses, in gardens and cultivated fields where they feed on grass seeds.

Poison Arrow Frogs are brightly coloured terrestrial frogs found in the rain forests of Central and South America from Costa Rica to southern Brazil where they live in dense vegetation with high humidity and running water. Native Americans hunted birds and monkeys with darts and arrows coated with the frogs' skin secretions, which are highly potent nerve toxins. There are 116 species of Poison-Arrow frog with colours varying from bright green to red, pink and gold. These bright colours warn potential predators, such as birds that normally eat frogs, to avoid the species. Poison-Arrow Frogs eat the tiniest of insects such as ants, termites and small spiders.

The Southern Boobook Owl is the smallest owl in Australia. It has brown plumage, with brown or buff underside and darker feathers around the eye area, giving the impression of a mask. They are seen in a variety of habitats from dense forest to open desert. Like other owl species, the Southern Boobook is nocturnal. They are often observed perched on an open branch or treetop, emitting a distinctive "boobook" or "mopoke" sound, and fly only to nest or feed. The Southern Boobook feeds on insects and other small animal species. Once detected, flying prey such as moths and small bats, are seized in mid-air, but most of their diet is ground-dwelling prey that is pounced upon. Boobooks are sedentary (perched) 95% of the time and are the ultimate "perch potatoes".

The Tropical Screech Owl is small with short ear tufts that are raised mostly during daytime. They are grey-brown in colour. This owl has a light gray facial disk, with a prominent black border. They eat insects such as crickets, katydids, beetles, ants, spiders and scorpions. They are found throughout much of South America.

The Egyptian Fruit Bat lives in a variety of habitat, from lowlands to mountains but determining factors are the presence of fruit to eat, and caves for roosting. Fruit bats have greyish-brown coats with a lighter shade on the stomach. They have short, strong jaws, a wingspan of about 24 inches, are four to seven inches in length, and weigh up to six ounces. Bats are nocturnal, and they find their way in the dark using high-pitched sounds, a process called echolocation. Fruit bats may fly 25 miles from roosting site in search of food.

Dwarf Caiman are found in Central and South America in semi aquatic areas, living in swamps, ponds and lakes; they are nocturnal. They eat fish, crustaceans, crabs, mollusks and shrimp. Males are about 4½ feet long and females around 4 feet. The young are brown in colour with blank banding, with the adults being darker. They have a unique shaped head, short and smooth. The upper jaw overlaps the lower. The skin is tough. Heavy scales cover the back as well as the belly, serving as protection due to their small size. The females use mounds for egg laying, which are usually made of mud and are hidden. The sex of the offspring is determined by the incubation temperature within the nest. High temperatures produce males, while females are produced in low temperatures.

The Blue and Gold Macaw has beautiful colouration with its back and upper tail feathers a brilliant blue and the underside of the tail an olive yellow. The forehead feathers are green, the wing feathers are blue with green tips, and the underwing and breast are yellow-orange. The bare facial area is creamy white with several lines made of small black feathers. The Blue and Gold Macaw measures between 32 and 35 inches long including its tail, has a three and a half foot wingspan, and weighs between 900 and 1200 grams. They are commonly found throughout Mexico, Central America, and the northern parts of South America living in rainforests, high in trees along swamps and rivers. Their diet consists of fruits, vegetable matter, seeds, nuts, leaves and bark, and some small animal life.

The Green Crested Turaco is found in the forests of tropical Africa. They are 43 centimetres long, including a long tail. Their plumage is green except for the small but thick red bill and red and white eye patches. They feed on fruit and blossoms.

The Red Crested Turaco is native to most parts of Africa. They eat over-ripe, mushy banana and papaya fruit. They love the water.

The Chestnut-mandibilled Toucan is native to most parts of Central America where they dwell in the trees in the moist lowland forests. They eat fruits, insects, lizards, bird eggs and other small prey. Toucans are one of the noisiest jungle birds, with a croak like a frog that can be heard for half a mile. The colourful beak of the Toucan is very light, made mostly of keratin (like fingernails), supported with thin rods of bone.

The Collared Aracari is a toucan which breeds in lowland forests and woodlands from Mexico to Panama. The head and chest is black, the upperparts are dark olive green, while the rump and upper tail are red. The under parts are bright yellow, with a round black spot in the centre of the breast and a red-tinted black band across the belly. They primarily eat fruit, but will also eat insects, lizards, bird eggs, and other small prey.

The Pied Imperial Pigeon is a widespread breeding bird on small islands adjoining the Indian Ocean where they are found in rainforests, eucalyptus woodland, coastal scrubs, creeks, rivers, and mangroves. They feed on fruit.

Pied Imperial Pigeon – very tame

The Eastern Rosella is native to Australia and is one of the best known parrots with its brilliantly coloured feathers of reds, yellows, greens and blues. It is up to 12 inches in total length. They prefer lightly timbered country (open forest, woodland, riverine forest, farmlands and towns). They feed on seeds, nectar fruit, insects and insect larvae. While most birds have three toes facing forward and one back, parrots have two of their four toes facing back which allows them to grasp and handle objects with dexterity.

The family Rallidae is a large group of small to medium-sized birds which includes the rails. Nearly all members are associated with wetlands with reed beds being a favoured habitat. Most species walk and run vigorously on strong legs, and have long toes which are well adapted to soft, uneven surfaces. They tend to have short, rounded wings and are weak fliers, although capable of covering long distances. The Giant Wood Rail is native to eastern South America. It has olive upperparts, a chestnut hind neck and a black tail. The face and fore-neck are pale bluish grey and the flanks and upper breast are a delicate brownish pink.

The Scarlet Ibis is native to the tropical regions and rainforests of Central and Northern South America. They survive on a diet of insects, fish, seeds and fruit. They are 22 to 24 inches in length. The brilliant red colour of the bird comes from the pigments in the bodies of the crustaceans that it eats.

The Superb Starling is a very common bird found in Africa, a small but distinctive bird with metallic greens and blues on its chest, back and wings and duller black on top of its head. The chestnut belly is divided from the dark chest by a stripe of white. They live in woodland, thorny bush and acacia country as well as in close proximity to human habitation, even within cities.

A small South American wild duck, the Ringed Teal, is a pretty little bird. The drake has a rich chestnut back, pale grey flanks and a salmon-coloured breast speckled in black. A black band runs from the top of its head to the nape. Fast and agile flyers, Ringed Teal enjoy perching in trees well off the ground.

The Bearded Barbet is a member of the woodpecker family and is native to most parts of Africa, living in wooded areas. This stout bird averages ten inches in length and weighs between 2½ and 3½ ounces. It is fairly plump, with a short neck, large head and a short tail. The adult has a black crown, back, tail and breast band; the throat and belly are red and there is a yellow eye patch; the rump is white. The massive bill is very thick and yellow, and the well developed clump of hair-like bristles at its base gives it the appearance of having a beard. It uses its sharp beak to feed on insects and fruit, and also to pound holes in dead trees or stumps for its nest. Barbets are social birds and live in groups of four or five. In the wild, they eat fruits such as figs and garden fruits.

The Silver-cheeked Hornbill is a large bird between 75 to 80 centimetres in length. It has a very large creamy casque on the beak. The head is silver-grey and the rest of the plumage is black, except for a broad white stripe in the back. They are native to the evergreen forests of Africa where they feed on fruits, insects, birds' eggs and centipedes.

The Golden Pheasant is a game bird native to forests in mountainous areas of western China. The adult male is 90-105 centimetres in length, its tail accounting for two-thirds of the total length. It has a golden crest and rump and bright red body. The deep orange "cape" can be spread in display, appearing as an alternating black and orange fan that covers all of the face except its bright yellow eye, with a pinpoint black pupil. Despite the male's showy appearance, these hardy birds are very difficult to see in their natural habitat, which is dense, dark young conifer forests with sparse undergrowth. They feed on the ground on grain, leaves, berries, grubs, seeds and invertebrates, but roost in trees at night. While they can fly, they prefer to run; if startled, they can suddenly burst upwards at great speed. They can fly in short bursts, but are quite clumsy in flight and spend most of their time on the ground.

The Hunting Cissa or Green Magpie is a member of the Crow family. It is a vivid green in colour, with a thick black stripe from the bill, through the eyes, to the nape. The tail is long and tapered with white tips. This contrasts with the reddish fleshy eye rims, red bill and legs. The wing primaries are reddish maroon. It is native to India, China, Malaysia, Sumatra and Borneo in evergreen forests (including bamboo forests), clearings and scrub. This bird seeks food both on the ground and in trees, and takes a very high percentage of animal prey from invertebrates, small reptiles, mammals and young birds and eggs. It will also eat flesh from a recently killed carcass.

Chaco Chachalacas are large birds that reside in trees and are similar in general appearance to turkeys. They are native to Central America and Mexico and are regarded as game birds which are hunted for food and sport. They feed on fruit, insects and worms.

The White Cheeked Bulbul of the Himalayas of Asia are beautiful songsters. Bulbuls feed mainly on fruits and berries.

The Royal Starling has iridescent feathers with its body a bright metallic blue, its head a vivid green, and the breast and thighs are yellow but with a violet breast patch. It is 12-15 inches long with the long tail feathers accounting for half of the total length. Royal Starlings are found in north-east Africa in dry bush and thorn bush areas with acacia trees. They eat insects, spiders, snails, crabs and other small vertebrates.

Cuban Anoles are native to Cuba and the Caribbean Islands and are found in bushes, trees up to 15 feet tall, and on rock walls. Anoles are sometimes called "chameleons" due to their colour-changing ability, especially when severely stressed or ill when they turn dark brown. Their diet includes grubs, crickets, cockroaches, spiders, moths, any arthropod which will fit in their mouths.

Fairy bluebirds inhabit the forests of the Himalayas, northern India, Burma and Indochina. They feed on fruit and insects, being particularly fond of wild figs, and also eat some flower nectar.

The Javanese House is part of an original house, circa 1875, from the central part of the Island of Java. Javanese houses of the wealthy and aristocratic class in the 19th century were several buildings linked together within a walled compound. This was the central building of the compound that was reserved for formal meetings with important visitors and the spiritual heart of the home. The richness of the carving and the shape of the main roof indicate that this house was for a very important person.

Entirely hand carved out of solid teak, the house was constructed without nails. The front door on the Island of Java faces south, the symbolic direction of the sea. The arrangement and number of panels, the stacked central beams, the different levels of the building were all designed according to very strict beliefs that formed Javanese culture.

The Javanese belief system includes Hinduism, Buddhism and Islam, mingled with indigenous beliefs in both culture and architecture. Even today, when the Island of Java has a population of 100 million people, this belief system is still relevant in the process of design and building so that it is in harmony with nature. Site location, layout, dimensions of the building, the proper time to take action, and rituals preceding any action in building are all considered important.

In the Javanese House inside the Aviary, refreshments can be purchased.

The Australian Singing Crow is native to Australia, New
Guinea, and neighboring islands of Indonesia. It lives on the
edges of rainforest, open forest, woodlands and tall scrub,
coastal margins, ranges and gorges of arid areas, and in
human settlements. It feeds mainly on insects, fruit, seeds,
and carrion. It is considered an agricultural pest, as it feeds on
grain, peanuts, and fruit.

The male Mandarin is the most beautiful of all ducks with an iridescent crown extending to a long crest and chestnut cheeks. The breast is maroon with black and white vertical stripes; the abdomen and underside are white with gold and black flanks. The back and tail are olive brown, the upper tail coverts are blue/green, and the scapulars are iridescent blue. The outer tertials are orange and gold on the inner web and form a sail shape while the upper wing surface is mostly olive brown. This sail shape feature along with the white-eye stripe that extends from the bill and tapers toward the back of the head is the distinguishing feature of the male. The bill is red and they have whitish legs with yellow feet. The Mandarin Duck originated in China but can be found almost anywhere there is a suitable habitat. Mandarins prefer to live in woodlands next to water that has many trees with holes for nesting. They like mountain areas with streams, marshland and forests. The Mandarins eat seeds, acorns, grain, aquatic plants, insects, land snails and fish.

I hope you have enjoyed travelling with me all over the world to learn about animals both large and small, each having their unique characteristics. Many are endangered due to man's expansion into their habitats, or to excessive killing of the animals for some part of them (such as the tusks of elephants, or the buffalo hides of the American bison).

Look for the next volume in the series of The Life and Times of Barbara coming soon.